THE LITTLE BOOK OF COCKNEY RHYMING SLANG

Sid Finch

summersdale

THE LITTLE BOOK OF COCKNEY RHYMING SLANG

Summersdale Publishers Ltd
46 West Street
Chichester
West Sussex
PO19 1RP
UK

www.summersdale.com

Printed and bound in the Czech Republic

ISBN: 978-1-84953-760-5

Substantial discounts on bulk quantities of Summersdale books are available to corporations, professional associations and other organisations. For details contact Nicky Douglas by telephone: +44 (0) 1243 756902, fax: +44 (0) 1243 786300 or email: nicky@summersdale.com.

CONTENTS

What's a Cockney?

A true cockney is someone born within the sound of Bow Bells (St Mary-le-Bow Church in Cheapside, London).

St Mary-le-Bow Church

But in recent times, 'cockney' has been applied to those who live on the outskirts of London as well, provided they come from a cockney background or have a cockney accent. In particular, Leighton Buzzard, Luton and Essex towns such as Romford are known for their cockney accents.

What's Rhyming Slang?

Rhyming slang involves finding a saying or expression which rhymes with the original word and then using that expression instead of the word. Often the word that rhymes is omitted (making it very confusing for a non-cockney speaker!). For example, you are having a 'butchers' at this book (butcher's hook – look). Whether or not to omit the rhyming part depends on the context.

Who Uses Cockney Rhyming Slang?

Although it started in London's East End, snippets of cockney rhyming slang are used all over the country. This is largely due to a raised awareness of it through television and the media. *Only Fools and Horses, Steptoe and Son* and *Porridge* have all played their part in spreading slang throughout the country.

Is Cockney Rhyming Slang Dead?

Absolutely not! Not only is it still in use but hundreds of new phrases and words have been created in the last few years, though many of them betray their modern roots by being derived from celebrity names. For example, 'Ayrton Senna – tenner' and 'Pete Tong – wrong'.

In addition, there is a lot of cockney rhyming slang that we use without realising it. For instance, 'telling porkies' (pork pies – lies) and 'having a barney' (barn owl – row).

Different Types of Cockney Rhyming Slang

Classic: All the originals from the good ol' days. Think 'dog and bone' and 'apples and pears'.

Modern: More recently introduced slang. For example, 'Adrian Mole' and 'Winona Ryder'.

Mockney: Is it real, or just a load of pony? Lots of today's celebrities would have us believe they're pearly kings and queens, thanks to their use of rhyming slang – some are easier to Adam and Eve than others...

Aa

À la Mode – Code. *'Let's talk à la mode.'*

Abergavenny – Penny. *'I ain't got an Abergavenny.'*

Able and Willing – Shilling. *'I'm skint; lend me an able.'*

Ace of Spades – AIDS. *'He's been diagnosed with ace of spades.'*

Ache and Pain – Rain. *'I'm not goin' out in the ache and pain!'*

Acker Bilk – Milk. *'I take Acker in my Rosie.'*

Adam and Eve – Believe. *'Can you Adam and Eve it?'*

Adam and the Ants – Pants. *'This is so Adam.'*

Adam Faith – Safe. *'Better keep your bees and honey in the Adam Faith.'*

Aa

Adrian Mole – Dole. *'I'm on the Adrian Mole.'*

Advice from Mother – Rubber (contraception). *'I hope you used advice from mother.'*

Ain't it a Treat – Street. *'I'm walking down the ain't it a treat.'*

Air Force – Sauce. *'More air force on your chips?'*

Air Gunner – Stunner. *'She was a right air gunner!'*

Air Miles – Piles (haemorrhoids). *'I've got a terrible case of air miles.'*

Airs and Graces – Braces. *'Better attach your airs and graces if you don't want your Callards to fall down.'*

A. J. Hackett – Jacket. *'I'll just grab my A. J. Hackett.'*

Al Capone – Telephone. *'Call me on the Al Capone.'*

Al Caponed – Stoned. *'Are we getting Al Caponed tonight?'*

Al Murray – Curry. *'Fancy an Al Murray?'*

Al Pacino – Cappuccino. *'Can you get me an Al Pacino?'*

Alan Border – Out of Order. *'That is so Alan Border!'*

Alan Knott – Hot. *'It ain't half Alan Knott in here.'*

Alan Ladd – Bad. *'That's well Alan!'*

Alan Minter – Splinter. *'I got an Alan in my finger!'*

Alan Pardew – Flu. *'I can't come out mate; I've got the Alan.'*

Alan Stringer – Minger. *'Those birds were a right pair of Alans.'*

Alan Whicker – Nicker (£1). *'Lend us an Alan.'*

Alan Whickers – Knickers. *'I can't find my Alan Whickers.'*

Albert Halls – Balls. *'I got kicked in the Alberts.'*

Alderman's Nail – Tail. *'That Andrew Marr's been on my Alderman's nail for a mile now.'*

Alex Nash – Slash (to urinate). *'I need an Alex.'*

Alexander Hleb – Pleb. *'You're a right Alexander.'*

Alexei Sayle – Email. *'Send us an Alexei Sayle with the details.'*

Alf Garnett – Barnet (hair). *'Gotta get my Alf Garnett cut.'*

Alger Hiss – Piss. *'I need an Alger.'*

Ali G – Pee. *'I'm going for an Ali G.'*

Ali McGraw – Score. *'What's the Ali?'*

Alibi Ike – Bike. *'On your Alibi Ike!'*

Alice Bands – Hands. *'It's in my Alice bands!'*

All Behind – Blind. *'He went all behind.'*

All-Night Rave – Shave. *'You'd better all-night rave for the interview.'*

All-Time Loser – Boozer (pub). *'I'll be down the all-time loser.'*

Alligator – Later. *'See ya alligator.'*

Almond Rocks – Socks. *'Put your almonds on!'*

Alphonse – Ponce. *'What an Alphonse.'*

Anchor Spreadable – Incredible. *'That's bloody Anchor Spreadable!'*

Ancient Greek – Freak. *'What an ancient Greek.'*

Andrew Marr – Car. *'I'll take the Andrew Marr.'*

Andy Cole – Goal. *'What an Andy Cole!'*

Andy Farley – Charlie (cocaine). *'I'm on the Andy Farley.'*

Andy McNab – Cab (taxi). *'I'll grab an Andy McNab.'*

Aa

Andy McNabs – Crabs. *'I've got a bad case of the Andy McNabs.'*

Andy Pandy – Dandy. *'He's a right Andy.'*

Anneka Rice – Price. *'If the Anneka is right.'*

Angela Merkel – Circle. *'We're goin' in Angela Merkels.'*

Angus MacGyver – Skiver. *'You're a right Angus MacGyver.'*

Ann Boleyn – Gin. *'If you reach the pub before me, get me an Anny.'*

Annie May Wong – Strong. *'I like my Rosie Annie May.'*

Ant 'n' Dec – Cheque. *'I'll take an Ant 'n' Dec.'*

Ant 'n' Decs – Oral Sex. *'Got some Ant 'n' Decs last night.'*

Anthea Turner – Earner. *'It's a right good Anthea Turner.'*

Anthony Blunt – Cunt. *'Stop bein' an Anthony!'*

Antiseptic – Anti-American (derived from Septic Tank – Yank). *'I'm antiseptic.'*

Apple Bobbing – Robbing. *'He's apple bobbing you blind mate!'*

Apple Cider – Spider. *'Get that apple cider away from me!'*

Apple Fritter – Bitter (beer). *'I'll have a pint of apple fritter.'*

Apple Pie – Sky. *'Stop starin' at the apple pie.'*

Apple Pip – Dip. *'Fancy an apple pip?'*

Apples and Pears – Stairs. *'Up the apples and pears.'*

April Fool – Tool. *'Hand us that April.'*

April Fools – Stools. *'Then 'e threw an April fool at me!'*

April Showers – Flowers. *'Get 'er some April showers and it'll be fine.'*

Aa

Arabian Nights – Shites. *'I 'ad the Arabians all night.'*

Aristotle – Bottle. *'Been on the Aristotle?'*

Army and Navy – Gravy. *'Pass the army.'*

Arnold Palmer – Farmer. *'He's an Arnold Palmer.'*

Artful Dodger – Lodger. *'Got an Artful Dodger stayin' at the moment.'*

Arthur Ashe – Cash. *'Just got to get some Arthur Ashe out.'*

Arthur Bliss – Piss. *'Just goin' for an Arthur.'*

Arthur Conan Doyle – Boil. *'Get the kettle on the Arthur.'*

Attila the Hun – Two-one (upper second-class degree). *'She got an Attila.'*

Aunt Mabel – Table. *'Mind yer manners at the Aunt Mabel.'*

Auntie Ella – Umbrella. *'Looks grey, better take my Auntie Ella.'*

Aunt Nell – Smell. *'What's that Aunt Nell?'*

Auntie Nelly – Telly. *'Anything on the Auntie Nelly?'*

Austin Power – Shower. *'Just jumpin' in the Austin.'*

Ave Maria – Fire. *'There's been an Ave Maria.'*

Ayers Rock – Cock. *'Don't be such an Ayers Rock.'*

Aylesbury Duck – Fuck. *'What the Aylesbury?'*

Ayrton Senna – Tenner (£10). *'Lend us an Ayrton.'*

Bb

Baa Lamb – Tram. *'I remember the days of baa lambs.'*

Babbling Brook – Crook. *'She's a bit of a babbling brook.'*

Babe Ruth – Truth. *'Ain't it the babe?'*

Baby Giraffe – Half (a pint). *'Just a baby giraffe for me tonight.'*

Bacardi Breezer – Geezer. *'You're a right Bacardi.'*

Bacon and Eggs – Legs. *'I can't feel my bacon and eggs!'*

Baked Potato – Later. *'See you baked potato.'*

Ball of Chalk – Walk. *'Let's go for a ball of chalk.'*

Balloon Car – Saloon Bar. *'We walked into this balloon car...'*

Band of Hope – Soap. *'Bloody hell, I've dropped the band of hope...'*

Bangers and Mash – Cash. *'Gis the bangers and mash then.'*

Barn Owl – Row (quarrel). *'They've been having a bit of a barney.'*

Barnaby Rudge – Judge. *'You can be the Barnaby Rudge of that.'*

Barnet Fair – Hair. *'Look at that fella's Barnet!'*

Barney Rubble – Trouble. *'We're in a whole heap of Barney.'*

Barry McGuigan – Big 'Un (big one). *'He's a Barry.'*

Basil Fawlty – Balti. *'Fancy a Basil Fawlty tonight?'*

Basin of Gravy – Baby. *'They're 'avin' a basin.'*

Bat and Wicket – Ticket. *'I've got the bat and wickets.'*

Bath Bun – Sun. *'Nice that the Bath bun's out today.'*

Battle Cruiser – Boozer (pub). *'See you down the battle tonight eh?'*

Battle of Waterloo – Stew. *'I'll 'ave the Battle of Waterloo.'*

Bear's Paw – Saw. *'Hand us the bear's paw.'*

Becks and Posh – Nosh (food). *'Just nippin' out for a bit of Becks and Posh.'*

Beecham's Pill – Bill (statement)/Still. *'Gotta pay the Beecham's.'*

Bees and Honey – Money. *'I'm good for the bees and honey.'*

Beetles and Ants – Underpants. *'I was down to my beetles!'*

Beggar-My-Neighbour – Labour. *'That's cheap beggar.'*

Bended Knees – Cheese. *'Get the bended knees out the fridge would ya?'*

Bengal Lancer – Chancer. *'Bit of a Bengal if you ask me.'*

Big Ben – Ten. *'He arrived just before Big Ben.'*

Big Dippers – Slippers. *'Where's my big dippers?'*

Billy Goat – Coat. *'Let me just put my billy on.'*

Bird Lime – Time. *'You got the bird?'*

Biscuits and Cheese – Knees. *'I was on my biscuits!'*

Bladder of Lard – Card. *'Better get a bladder of lard.'*

Bo-Peep – Sleep. *'I got no Bo last night.'*

Bb

Boat Race – Face. *'Punched me right in the boat!'*

Bob Hope – Soap. *'Pass the Bob.'*

Bob Squash – Wash. *'I'll just have a Bob.'*

Bobby Moore – Sure. *'Are you Bobby?'*

Bonney Fair – Hair. *'She's havin' her Bonney Fair styled.'*

Bonnie and Clyde – Snide. *'She was a bit Bonnie with me.'*

Boracic Lint – Skint. *'I'm boracic at the moment mate!'*

Borrow and Beg – Egg. *'We need to get some borrow and begs.'*

Botany Bay – Run Away. *'I wanted to Botany Bay.'*

Bottle and Glass – Class. *'Top of the bottle and glass.'*

Bottle and Stopper – Copper (police). *'Oi oi, 'ere come the bottle an' stoppers!'*

Bottle of Cola – Bowler (hat). *'Strollin' along, wearing a bottle of cola!'*

Bottle of Porter – Daughter. *'This is my bottle of porter.'*

Bottle of Sauce – Horse. *'They were riding a bottle of sauce.'*

Bottle of Scotch – Wristwatch. *"Ave you seen my new bottle of scotch?'*

Bow and Arrow – Para (paranoid). *'No need to get bow.'*

Box of Toys – Noise. *'There was a right box of toys coming from it.'*

Brass Band – Hand. *'Take my brass band.'*

Brass Tacks – Facts. *'Let's 'ave the brass tacks.'*

Bread and Butter – Gutter. *'Sleepin' in the bread and butter.'*

Bb

Bread and Honey – Money. *'I've got the bread.'*

Bricks and Mortar – Daughter. *'That's my bricks and mortar.'*

Bright and Breezy – Easy. *'Bright an' breezy now.'*

Briney Marlin – Darling. *'Alright Briney?'*

Britney Spears – Beers. *'I'll bring the Britneys.'*

Brixton Riot – Diet. *'I'm on a Brixton Riot at the mo.'*

Brothers and Sisters – Whiskers. *'Trim yer brothers and sisters.'*

Brown Bread – Dead. *'He's brown bread.'*

Brown Hat – Cat. *'We've got a brown hat.'*

Brussels Sprout – Nowt. *'I've got Brussels.'*

Bubble and Squeak – Week. *'See you in a bubble and squeak.'*

Bucket and Pail – Jail. *'I could go to bucket and pail.'*

Buddy Holly – Volley. *'Buddy that over 'ere.'*

Bugs Bunny – Money. *'I got no Bugs Bunny.'*

Bullock's Horn – Pawn. *'Did you bullock's horn it?'*

Burnt Cinder – Window. *'I 'ad to climb out the burnt cinder!'*

Burton-on-Trent – Rent. *'I've paid the Burton.'*

Bushel and Peck – Neck. *'It's around my bushel.'*

Bushy Park – Lark (joke). *'It's only a Bushy Park!'*

Buster Keaton – Meeting. *'I've got a Buster Keaton then.'*

Butcher's Hook – Look. *'Let's 'ave a butchers.'*

Cc

Cab Rank – Bank. *'I gotta go to the cab rank.'*

Cain and Abel – Table. *'Put 'em on the Cain and Abel.'*

Callard and Bowsers – Trousers. *'My Callards are too big!'*

Calvin Klein – Fine. *'That's Calvin with me, mate.'*

Captain Hook – Book. *'It was in that Captain Hook.'*

Cash and Carried – Married. *'They're getting' cash 'n' carried this year.'*

Cat and Cages – Wages. *'I get my cat 'n' cages on Friday.'*

Cat and Mouse – House. *'Pop by my cat and mouse later.'*

Cellar Flap – Tap (to ask for a loan). *'I need to cellar flap a Lady Godiva.'*

Chalfont St Giles – Piles (haemorrhoids). *'I've got a case of the Chalfont St Giles.'*

Chalk Farm – Arm. *'I've got a new tattoo on my Chalk Farm.'*

Charles Fox – Box. *'What's in the Charles Fox then?'*

Charlie Chan – Tan. *'That's a pretty nice Charlie you've got there.'*

Charlie Prescot – Waistcoat. *'Nice Charlie Prescot.'*

Charlie Pride – Ride. *'Want to go for a Charlie?'*

Chas and Dave – Shave. *'I need a Chas and Dave.'*

Cheerful Giver – Liver. *'You'll ruin your cheerful giver if you carry on tumblin' down the sink like this.'*

Cc

Cheese and Kisses – Missus. *'Where's the cheese and kisses?'*

Cheggers Plays Pop – Shop. *'Just popping down the Cheggers.'*

Cheltenham Bold – Cold. *'It's a bit Cheltenham in 'ere.'*

Cherry Hog – Dog. *'The bloody cherry was barkin' all night.'*

Chevy Chase – Face. *'Say that to my Chevy!'*

Chew the Fat – Chat. *'Come over and we'll chew the fat.'*

Chicken and Rice – Nice. *'This is pretty chicken and rice.'*

China Plate – Mate (friend). *'My ol' China.'*

Chipmunks – Trunks. *'I'm in my chipmunks!'*

Chocolate Fudge – Judge. *'I'll be the chocolate fudge of that!'*

Christian Slater – Later. *'See ya Christian.'*

Christmas Eve – Believe. *'I don't Christmas Eve it!'*

Cilla Black – Back. *'My Cilla's gone!'*

Claire Raynor – Trainer. *'I'll just put my Claire Raynors on.'*

Clever Mike – Bike. *'Been ridin' round town on a clever Mike.'*

Clickety Click – Sixty-six. *'There's only clickety click days left until your birthday, son!'*

Clothes Peg – Egg. *'For breakfast I had clothes peg and holy ghost.'*

Coals and Coke – Broke (financially ruined). *'I'd love to come down the Jack Tar, but I'm coals and coke.'*

Coat and Badge – Cadge (borrow). *'Coat us a deep sea diver.'*

Cock and Hen – Ten. *'I'll be back before you count to cock and hen.'*

Cc

Cock Linnet – Minute. *'Gimme a cock linnet!'*

Cock Sparrow – Barrow. *'I've hurt my Jumping Jack pushing around this cock sparrow.'*

Cockroach – Coach. *'I'll be drivin' the cockroach.'*

Conan Doyle – Boil. *'I've got an awful Conan Doyle on my these and those.'*

Country Cousin – Dozen. *'Half a country cousin of one, Tom Mix of the other.'*

Cow's Calf – Half (fifty pence). *'I'm a cow's calf short for my kidney punch.'*

Cream Cookies – Bookies. *'I'm off down the cream cookies to put some money on a bottle of sauce.'*

Cream Crackered – Knackered. *'I'm absolutely cream crackered.'*

Crust of Bread – Head. *'I smacked my crust of bread on the Rory O'Moore.'*

Cuddle and Kiss – Miss. *'Aren't you a fancy little cuddle and kiss?'*

Currant Bun – Sun. *'The currant bun is shining right in my mince pies.'*

Currant Cakey – Shaky. *'I'm feeling a bit currant cakey after my heavy night on the River Ouse.'*

Custard and Jelly – Telly. *'What's on the custard tonight?'*

Cuts and Scratches – Matches. *'You got any cuts and scratches so I can light my Harry Wragg?'*

Dd

Daff-a-Down Dilly – Silly. *'Don't be so daff-a-down dilly!'*

Daft and Barmy – Army. *'He left Ja Rule to join the daft and barmy.'*

Daily Mail – Tale. *'Did you think I'd believe that Daily Mail?'*

Daisy Roots – Boots. *'These daisy roots are too small for my plates of meat.'*

Dancing Fleas – Keys. *'Have you got my dancing fleas in your Lucy locket?'*

Danny La Rue – Clue. *'I ain't got a Danny La Rue.'*

Danny Marr – Car. *'He wanted me to have Oedipus Rex in the Danny Marr!'*

Darky Cox – Box. *'We went to the theatre and sat in a Darky Cox.'*

David Gower – Shower. *'I had to take a David Gower to get rid of the Aunt Nell.'*

Day and Night – Light (ale). *'Just a pint of day and night for me.'*

Day's Dawning – Morning. *'In the day's dawning I felt proper Tom and Dick.'*

Deep Sea Diver – Fiver (£5). *'Hey mate, you dropped a deep sea diver!'*

Derby Kelly – Belly. *'I need to get down the Fat Boy Slim to get rid of this derby kel.'*

Derry and Tom – Bomb. *'He's in the daft and barmy as an expert on Derry and Toms.'*

Dd

Dick Emery – Memory. *'Now I'm getting on a bit I'm losing my Dick Emery.'*

Dickie Bird – Word. *'I ain't heard a Dickie Bird.'*

Dickory Dock – Clock. *'Could you take a look at that dickory dock and let me know the Harry Lime?'*

Dicky Dirt – Shirt. *'I need to Bob Squash my dicky.'*

Dig in the Grave – Shave. *'He'd look a lot nicer if he had a dig in the grave.'*

Ding Dong – Song. *'I learnt this old sea ding dong when I was in the soup and gravy.'*

Ding Dong Bell – Hell. *'When she was angry she'd really give them ding dong bell.'*

Dixie Deans – Jeans. *'His dixie deans were soaked in Arthur.'*

Doctor Crippen – Dripping. *'A lovely dinner of Uncle Fred and Doctor Crippen.'*

Dog and Bone – Telephone. *'Call me on the dog and bone.'*

Donkey's Ears – Years. *'I haven't been there in donkeys!'*

Dot and Dash – Moustache. *'That's a crackin' dot and dash!'*

Doug McClure – Whore. *'I'm not one to gossip, but he was a bit of a Doug McClure.'*

Down the Drains – Brains. *'She's the one with all the down the drains.'*

Dribs and Drabs – Crabs. *'What's the matter, got dribs and drabs?'*

Drum and Fife (shortened to Drummond) – Knife. *'You'll need a sharper Drummond.'*

Drummond and Roce – Knife and Fork. *'No manners, that boy. He won't even use a Drummond and Roce!'*

Duchess of Fife – Wife. *'I'll pop in the Mickey Mouse and ask the Duchess.'*

Duck and Dive – Hide. *'This is a great place to duck and dive!'*

Dudley Moore – Sore. *'I cycled so far, my Khyber Pass was Dudley Moore.'*

Duke of Argyles – Piles (haemorrhoids). *'With these Duke of Argyles, I need to sit on a tit willow.'*

Duke of Kent – Rent. *'We need that sugar and honey to pay the Duke of Kent!'*

Duke of York – Chalk. *'This soil is full of Duke of York!'*

Dunlop Tyre – Liar. *'Are you calling me a Dunlop?!'*

Dustbin Lid – Kid (child). *'Aw, leave him alone; he's only a dustbin!'*

Ee

Early Doors – Drawers (pair of). *'He dropped his early doors and took an Alger Hiss on my front door!'*

Early Hours – Flowers. *'He said he was sorry and gave me a bunch of early hours.'*

Earwig – Twig (to understand). *'He didn't earwig we were all having a Turkish at him.'*

East and West – Vest. *'I've gone and spilt loop the loop on my east and west.'*

Eddie Grundies – Undies. *'Of course you're cold, you're in your Eddie Grundies!'*

Eighteen Pence – Sense. *'He was so tired he wasn't making any eighteen pence!'*

Elephant and Castle – Parcel. *'It cost me a bleedin' fortune to post that elephant and castle!'*

Elephant's Trunk – Drunk. *'I was so elephant's, I could hardly rabbit and pork!'*

Elsie Tanner – Spanner. *'Pass me the Elsie Tanner.'*

Emma Freuds – Haemorrhoids. *'Can you get me some cream for my Emma Freuds?'*

Engineers and Stokers – Brokers. *'He thinks he's one of them engineers and stokers down the stock exchange.'*

Ernie Marsh – Grass. *'I skidded on the Ernie Marsh and fell off my clever Mike.'*

Ff

Fanny Craddock – Haddock. *'D'you want peas with your Fanny Craddock?'*

Far East – Priest. *'The vicar said he'll speak to the Far East.'*

Farmer Giles – Piles (haemorrhoids). *'My Farmer Giles are driving me mum and dad!'*

Fat Boy Slim – Gym. *'Just goin' down the Fat Boy Slim.'*

Feather and Flip – Kip (sleep). *'Don't make too much box of toys, I need to get some feather and flip.'*

Field of Wheat – Street. *'I parked my car on the field of wheat.'*

Fine and Dandy – Brandy. *'He'll be alright after a nip of fine and dandy.'*

Ff

Finger and Thumb – Rum. *'Pass me the bottle of finger and thumb.'*

Fish Hook – Book. *'He's got his nose in a fish hook again.'*

Fisherman's Daughter – Water. *'We ran out of fisherman's daughter; I thought I'd die of Geoff Hurst!'*

Flounder and Dab – Cab (taxi). *'Quick, we're late, get in the flounder!'*

Flowery Dell – Cell (prison). *'I spent nine years in that flowery dell.'*

Fly-by-Nights – Tights. *'I've got another ladder in my fly-by-nights!'*

Fore and Aft – Daft. *'Don't be fore and aft!'*

Fork and Knife – Wife. *'I'm gettin' strife from my fork and knife.'*

Forsyte Saga – Lager. *'He didn't want a finger and thumb, so I got him a Forsyte.'*

Frank Bough – Off. *'That's a bit Frank Bough!'*

Fridge Freezer – Geezer. *'I hear he's a bit of a fridge freezer.'*

Frog and Toad – Road. *'Drive down the frog and toad and turn right into the next field of wheat.'*

Frying Pan – Old Man (husband). *'My frying pan's been banged up in a flowery dell.'*

Gg

Garden Gate – Mate (friend). *'You can have it for a fiver, seein' as you're a garden gate.'*

Gary Ablett – Tablet. *'Pass me the Gary Abletts; my knee's givin' me gip again.'*

Gates of Rome – Home. *'There's no place like the Gates of Rome.'*

Gay and Frisky – Whisky. *'Ice in your gay and frisky?'*

Geoff Hurst – Thirst. *'This'll quench your Geoff Hurst.'*

George Raft – Draught. *'Is it me or can you feel a George Raft?'*

German Band – Hand. *'Get your Germans off my missus!'*

Gertie Gitana – Banana. *'I always eat a Gertie before going to the Fat Boy Slim.'*

Ginger Beer – Engineer. *'You'll need to call out a ginger beer.'*

Gipsy's Warning – Morning. *'It's a beaut of a gipsy's warning!'*

Giraffe – Laugh. *'I'm tellin' you, we had a right giraffe.'*

Glasgow Ranger – Stranger. *'Never seen him before; he's a complete Glasgow Ranger.'*

God Forbid – Kid (child). *'Watch out for that God forbid!'*

Gold Watch – Scotch. *'Make mine a double gold watch.'*

Goose's Neck – Cheque. *'I paid my goose's neck into the tin tank.'*

Gg

Gooseberry Pudding – Woman. *'That gooseberry pudding'll be the death of me!'*

Gordon and Gotch – Wrist Watch. *'Where d'ya get your Gordon and Gotch?'*

Grass in the Park – Nark. *'I'm not a grass!'*

Grasshopper – Copper (police). *'I turned him over to the grasshopper.'*

Greengages – Wages. *'That's done it, I've gone and blown all my greens!'*

Gregory Peck – Neck. *'I'm always gettin' it in the Gregory Peck.'*

Grey Mare – Fare. *'How much is the grey mare?'*

Hh

Ha'penny Dip – Ship. *'He set sail in his ha'penny dip.'*

Hackney Marsh – Glass. *'Let me top up your Hackney Marsh.'*

Haddock and Bloater – Motor. *'I've just bought a new haddock and bloater.'*

Half a Gross – Dose. *'It's not working; try doubling the half a gross.'*

Half Inch – Pinch (to steal). *'Are you sure you didn't half inch it?'*

Ham and Cheesy – Easy. *'Told you it was ham and cheesy!'*

Ham and Eggs – Legs. *'I've got bruises all over my ham and eggs!'*

Hh

Ham Shank – Yank. *'It'll come off, just give it a good ham shank.'*

Hammer and Tack – Back. *'My hammer and tack's gone, I'm in a right Harry Tate!'*

Hampstead Heath – Teeth. *'Gotta go down the dentist to have my Hampstead looked at.'*

Hank Marvin – Starving. *'I'm so Hank Marvin.'*

Harold Wilsons – Stilsons (pipe wrenches). *'Can you lend me your Harolds?'*

Harpers and Queens – Jeans. *'What do you think of my new Harpers and Queens?'*

Harry Dash – Flash. *'Quick as a Harry Dash!'*

Harry Lime – Time. *'My old man's inside, doing Harry Lime.'*

Harry Lin – Chin. *'She caught me right on my Harry Lin!'*

Harry Randall – Candle. *'Another power cut! Where are the Harry Randalls?'*

Harry Tate – Eight. *'I'll be there at a quarter past Harry Tate.'*

Harry Wragg – Fag (cigarette). *'He's smoking a Harry Wragg.'*

Harvey Nichol – Pickle. *'We're in a right Harvey Nichol!'*

Hatti Jacques – Shakes. *'She's got the Hatti Jacques.'*

Heap of Coke – Bloke. *'He's a decent heap.'*

Hearts of Oak – Broke (financially ruined). *'We're totally hearts of oak.'*

Hedge and Ditch – Pitch (stall or stand). *'I'm gonna sell Sexton Blakes on my hedge and ditch.'*

Henry Moore – Door. *'There's a lemon squeezer at the Henry Moore...'*

Hh

Herring and Kipper – Stripper. *'He's gone on a date with that herring and kipper.'*

Hey Diddle Diddle – Fiddle. *'I played my hey diddle diddle.'*

Highland Fling – Ring. *'He spent all his greens on a diamond highland fling.'*

Hillman Hunters – Punters. *'It's gonna be a good day; there's lots of Hillman Hunters.'*

Hit and Miss – Kiss. *'The cheek of it; that heap just asked me for a hit and miss!'*

Hobson's Choice – Voice. *'I've lost my Hobson's.'*

Holy Friar – Liar. *'I'm not saying you're a Holy Friar, but someone half inched it.'*

Holy Ghost – Toast. *'Would you like some tea with your Holy Ghost?'*

Horse and Cart – Heart. *'It broke my horse and cart.'*

Hot Cross Bun – Nun. *'It's rare to see a hot cross bun round here.'*

Hot Potato – Waiter. *'Call the hot potato over.'*

House to Let – Bet. *'I put on a small house to let.'*

Housemaid's Knee – Sea. *'My dream is to live by the housemaid's knee.'*

How Do You Do – Shoe. *'I need new how do you dos.'*

How's Your Father – Lather. *'Work up a good how's your father.'*

I Suppose – Nose. *'Blow your I suppose.'*

I'm Afloat – Overcoat. *'I'm wearing my new I'm afloat.'*

Ice-Cream Freezer – Geezer. *'He's not a bad old ice cream.'*

In and Out – Gout. *'I've got in and out in my these and those.'*

In the Nude – Food. *'I'm going shopping for some in the nude.'*

Inky Smudge – Judge. *'That inky smudge looks funny in his Irish.'*

Insects and Ants – Underpants. *'I'm wearin' my thermal insects.'*

Irish Jig – Wig. *'I'm sure that bird's Barnet is an Irish.'*

Irish Rose – Nose. *'You've got something on your Irish rose.'*

Iron Horse – Toss (care). *'I don't give an iron mate!'*

Iron Tank – Bank. *'Just got to deposit a Gregory in the ol' iron.'*

Isle of Wight – Right. *'I knew I was Isle of Wight!'*

Itch and Scratch – Match. *'La-di-das are much nicer if you light 'em with an itch and scratch.'*

Ivory Band – Hand. *'Ouch, I've hurt my ivory!'*

Jj

J. Arthur Rank – Wank. *'The dirty bugger had a sly J. Arthur in the toilets!'*

Jack and Jill – Bill (statement)/Hill/Pill/Till. *'Not another Jack and Jill!'*

Jack Jones – Alone. *'I've been sat here all on my Jack.'*

Jack Tar – Bar (pub). *'See you at six in the Jack Tar.'*

Jack the Dandy – Brandy. *'I wouldn't say no to a Jack the Dandy.'*

Jack the Ripper – Kipper. *'Fancy a Jack the Ripper?'*

Jack's Alive – Five. *'I'm cream crackered; I've been up since Jack's alive!'*

Jackanory – Story (lie). *'Are you telling me a Jackanory?'*

Jackdaw – Jaw. *'My dentist says I'm clenching my jackdaw.'*

Jackdaw and Rook – Book. *'She's gone to Joe Brown to get a jackdaw and rook.'*

Ja Rule – School. *'I'll walk you to Ja Rule.'*

Jam Jar – Car. *'My jam jar's gone in for its MOT.'*

Jam Tart – Heart. *'She's been to the doctor about her jam tart.'*

Jam Tarts – Sweethearts. *'They were childhood jam tarts.'*

James Fox – Box. *'Look in the James Fox.'*

Jenny Lee – Flea. *'That dog of yours has caught Jenny Lees!'*

Jj

Jeremiah – Fire. *'Put some wood on the Jeremiah.'*

Jerry O'Gorman – Mormon. *'Didn't she marry a Jerry O'Gorman?'*

Jim Skinner – Dinner. *'Why don't you invite them over for Jim Skinner?'*

Jimmy O'Goblin – Sovereign. *'My grandad gave me a gold Jimmy O'Goblin.'*

Jimmy Riddle – Piddle. *'Just off for a Jimmy.'*

Joanna – Piano. *'Give us a tinkle on the ol' Joanna.'*

Joe Baxi – Taxi. *'I've booked us a Joe Baxi.'*

Joe Blake – Steak. *'You serve the best Jo Blake in the whole world!'*

Joe Brown – Town. *'This Joe Brown is too crowded for me.'*

Joe Hook – Book. *'I hear he's writing another Joe Hook.'*

Joe Rook – Crook (criminal). *'He's a Joe Rook, no doubt about it.'*

John Cleese – Cheese. *'Who wants toast with ham and John Cleese?'*

John Hop – Cop (police). *'Look out, it's the John Hops!'*

John Major – Wager. *'Let's settle this with a little John Major.'*

Johnnie Rutter – Butter. *'Pass me the Johnnie Rutter.'*

Johnny Horner – Corner. *'It's just round the Johnny Horner.'*

Jumping Jack – Back. *'My jumping jack's been killing me today!'*

Kk

Kate and Sydney – Steak and Kidney. *'We're 'aving Kate and Sydney pie.'*

Kate Carney – Army. *'He's in the Kate Carney.'*

Kate Mossed – Lost. *'Oh no, I think we're Kate Mossed!'*

Ken Dodd – Wad. *'He pulled out a Ken Dodd of banknotes.'*

Ken Smee – Pee. *'Stop the jam jar; I need to Ken Smee!'*

Kettle on the Hob – Fob (watch). *'Nice new kettle you got there, mate.'*

Khyber Pass – Arse. *'Stick that up your Khyber!'*

Kick and Prance – Dance. *'You want to go to the kick and prance tonight?'*

Kidney Punch – Lunch. *'I'm taking her out for kidney punch.'*

Kilkenny – Penny. *'If I had a Kilkenny for every time someone said that to me!'*

King Death – Breath. *'Take a deep king.'*

King Lears – Ears. *'Aw, look at his floppy King Lears!'*

Kippers – Slippers. *'Where are my kippers? My feet are cold.'*

La-Di-Da – Cigar. *'He's handing out la-di-das to celebrate the birth of his basin.'*

Lady Godiva – Fiver (£5). *'It's yours for a Lady mate.'*

Laugh and Titter – Bitter (beer). *'Fancy a pint of laugh and titter?'*

Left in the Lurch – Church. *'You gettin' married in the left in the lurch?'*

Lemon and Lime – Crime. *'I don't like this place; there's too much lemon and lime.'*

Lemon Squeezy – Easy. *'See, told you it was lemon squeezy!'*

Lemon Squeezer – Geezer. *'I blagged this la-di-da off that old lemon squeezer.'*

Leo Sayer – All-Dayer (drinking session). *'Me and the lads are planning a Leo Sayer.'*

Lester Piggot – Bigot. *'Don't let a few Lester Piggots ruin your day.'*

Light and Dark – Park. *'The kids are playin' football in the light and dark.'*

Lilley and Skinner – Beginner/Dinner. *'What did you have for your Lilley and Skinner?'*

Lillian Gish – Fish. *'Good day at the river; caught a couple of Lillians.'*

Linen Draper – Newspaper. *'It's all over the linen!'*

Lionel Bart – Fart. *'It stinks in here; did you let off a Lionel?'*

Lionel Blairs – Flares (wide trousers). *'I'm wearin' my Lionel Blairs.'*

LI

Loaf of Bread – Head. *'Use your loaf!'*

Lollipop – Shop (inform on). *'I reckon she lollipopped me to the John Hops.'*

Longers and Lingers – Fingers. *'Ain't you got big longers and lingers!'*

Loop the Loop – Soup. *'You got any Uncle Fred to go with this loop the loop?'*

Lord Lovell – Shovel. *'I'll try out my new Lord Lovell.'*

Lord Mayor – Swear. *'Don't you Lord Mayor at me!'*

Lousy Brown – Crown. *'Don't be stupid, you can't be a king without a lousy brown!'*

Love and Kisses – Missus. *'Just buying some April showers for my love and kisses.'*

Lucy Locket – Pocket. *'Keep it in your Lucy.'*

Lump of Lead – Head. *'Don't worry, it's all in my lump.'*

Mm

Macaroni – Pony (£25). *'Like these ones and twos? I only paid a macaroni.'*

Mae West – Best. *'My nan's the Mae West.'*

Major Loda – Soda. *'I'll have a lime and Major Loda.'*

Major Stevens – Evens (fifty-fifty bet). *'The odds are Major Stevens.'*

Man on the Moon – Spoon. *'Pass me a man on the moon and I'll serve up the Tommy Tucker.'*

Mangle and Wringer – Singer. *'She's a fantastic mangle and wringer.'*

Marbles and Conkers – Bonkers (mad). *'The whole world's gone marbles!'*

Master McGrath – Bra. *'I'm off to buy a new Master McGrath.'*

Mm

Me and You – Menu. *'Anything good on the me and you?'*

Merlyn Rees – Piece (lunch). *'I'm totally Hank Marvin – I skipped my Merlyn Rees.'*

Metric Miles – Piles (haemorrhoids). *'I'm 'aving terrible trouble with my metric miles.'*

Mickey Mouse – House. *'We need a bigger Mickey Mouse.'*

Microchip – Nip. *'That dog's a menace; he's just microchipped my Mystic Meg!'*

Mince Pies – Eyes. *'Ain't she got beautiful minces?'*

Moby Dick – Sick. *'I'm off work; I'm Moby Dick.'*

Molly O'Morgan – Organ. *'My cousin plays the Molly O'Morgan in the left in the lurch.'*

Monkey's Tail – Nail. *'Just attach it to the wall with a couple of monkey's tails.'*

Morecambe and Wise – Flies. *'Where have all these Morecambe and Wise come from?'*

Mork and Mindy – Windy. *'Don't give him Brussels sprouts again; he gets all Mork and Mindy.'*

Mortar and Trowel – Towel. *'Can you hand me a mortar for the Austin Power?'*

Mother Hubbard – Cupboard. *'The jam's in the Mother Hubbard.'*

Mother of Pearl – Girl. *'I'll run it by the old mother of pearl.'*

Mrs Duckett – Bucket. *'I think she's kicked the Mrs Duckett.'*

Mrs Chant – Aunt. *'Don't tell my Mrs Chant, she'll go Radio Rental!'*

Mum and Dad – Mad. *'He gets very mum and dad if you ignore him.'*

Mutt and Jeff – Deaf. *'What's that? I've gone a bit Mutt and Jeff.'*

Mm

Mutter and Stutter – Butter. *'My favourite breakfast is toast with mutter and stutter.'*

Mystic Megs – Legs. *'Sit down and take a load off your Mystic Megs.'*

Nn

Nails and Tacks – Fax. *'Can you nails and tacks it to me?'*

Nanny Goat – Boat. *'I took my nanny goat out on the river.'*

Near and Far – Bar (pub). *'Meet you for a needle and pin in the near and far?'*

Ned Kelly – Telly (television). *'What's on the Ned Kelly?'*

Needle and Pin – Gin. *'Do you want ice and lemon with your needle and pin?'*

Nelly Duff – Puff (breath, life). *'Not on your Nelly!'*

Nelson Eddys – Readies (ready money). *'My old man's got the Nelsons.'*

Nn

Nelson Mandelas – Stellas (beers). *'Nab a lion's lair and I'll get the Nelson Mandelas.'*

Nervo and Knox – Pox. *'Stay away, she's got the Nervo and Knox.'*

Nervous Wreck – Cheque. *'I'm waitin' for the nervous wreck to arrive.'*

Newgate Gaol – Tale. *'He was full of Newgates.'*

Newington Butts – Guts. *'My Newingtons are playin' up.'*

Night Boat to Cairo – Giro. *'She's gone to pick up her night boat.'*

Noah's Ark – Lark. *'Always one for a Noah's ark.'*

Nobby Stiles – Piles (haemorrhoids). *'It could be worse; you could have Nobby Stiles!'*

North and South – Mouth. *'How on earth did you miss your north and south?'*

Nuclear Sub – Pub. *'Every Friday he's down the nuclear sub.'*

Nuremberg Trials – Piles (haemorrhoids). *'I can't sit down cos of my Nurembergs.'*

Nutmegs – Legs. *'Cor, look at the nutmegs on that!'*

Oo

Obadiah – Fire. *'Ain't it lovely sitting by the Obadiah?'*

Ocean Pearl – Girl. *'She looks like a nice young ocean pearl.'*

Ocean Wave – Shave. *'A quick shower and an ocean wave and I'll be with you.'*

Oedipus Rex – Sex. *'I can't remember the last time I had Oedipus Rex.'*

Oily Rag – Fag (cigarette). *'Mate, can I scrounge an oily rag?'*

Oliver Twist – Fist. *'Before I knew it, his Oliver Twist was in my Chevy Chase!'*

On the Floor – Poor. *'I'm fed up with being so on the floor.'*

Once a Week – Cheek. *'Turn the other once a week.'*

One and the Other – Brother. *'My one and other feels a bit Pat and Mick.'*

One-Time Looker – Hooker (prostitute). *'Rumour has it she's a one-time looker.'*

Ones and Twos – Shoes. *'These ones and twos are too small for my plates of meat!'*

Oscar Asche – Cash. *'I'm a bit strapped for Oscar at the moment.'*

Oxford Scholar – Dollar (five shillings). *'Over there it will cost you an Oxford.'*

Oxo Cube – Tube (underground). *'It'll be quicker if you take the Oxo.'*

Pp

Paraffin Lamp – Tramp. *'He needs some new clothes; he looks like a paraffin.'*

Pat and Mick – Sick. *'The cat's just been Pat and Mick again!'*

Pat Malone – Alone. *'I'm all Pat Malone.'*

Pear Halved – Starved. *'Shall we have kidney punch in a bit? I'm pear halved!'*

Peas in the Pot – Hot. *'It's too peasy in 'ere.'*

Peckham Rye – Tie. *'Are you going to wear your new Peckham Rye?'*

Pen and Ink – Stink. *'What's that terrible pen and ink?'*

Penny-a-Pound – Ground. *'I found it on the penny.'*

Pete Tong – Wrong. *'It's all gone Pete Tong!'*

Peter Pan – Can (prison). *'He's off to the Peter Pan for a bit.'*

Piccadilly Percy – Mercy. *'Show him some Piccadilly Percy.'*

Piccolo and Flute – Suit. *'Does this Peckham Rye go with this piccolo?'*

Pick and Mix – Sticks (countryside). *'They've moved out to the pick and mix.'*

Pie and Mash – Flash. *'Quick as a pie and mash!'*

Pig's Ear – Beer. *'I'll have a pint of pig's ear mate.'*

Pimple and Blotch – Scotch. *'A bottle of your best pimple and blotch please, guv.'*

Pineapple – Chapel. *'You'll find the vicar in the pineapple.'*

Pp

Pineapple Chunk – Bunk. *'He's done a pineapple!'*

Pinky and Perky – Turkey. *'Do you want cranberry sauce with your Pinky and Perky?'*

Pipe Your Eye – Cry. *'Aw, don't pipe your eye!'*

Pitch and Toss – Boss. *'Right you are; you're the pitch and toss.'*

Pittsburgh Steelers – Peelers (police). *'I got nabbed by the Pittsburghs!'*

Plates and Dishes – Missus. *'I'm going pope in Rome to my plates and dishes.'*

Plates of Meat – Feet. *'My plates of meat are killin' me!'*

Pleasure and Pain – Rain. *'Is that a spot of pleasure and pain?'*

Plimsoll Mark – Park. *'Fancy a walk in the plimsoll mark?'*

Plink Plonk – Vin Blanc (wine). *'A bottle of plonk.'*

Pony and Trap – Crap. *'What a load of pony!'*

Pope in Rome – Home. *'I like what you've done with your pope in Rome!'*

Pork Pies – Lies. *'Are you telling me porkies?'*

Port and Brandy – Randy. *'I'm feelin' a bit port and brandy!'*

Pot and Pan – Man. *'That pot and pan has a very loud Rolls Royce!'*

Pot of Glue – Clue. *'I ain't got a pot of glue.'*

Potatoes in the Mould – Cold. *'It's really taters in 'ere!'*

Pots and Dishes – Wishes. *'Close your eyes and make a pot and dish.'*

Pull Down the Shutter – Butter. *'Pass me the pull down the shutter, would you?'*

Qq

Quaker Oat – Coat. *'Where's my Quaker Oat?'*

Rr

Rabbit and Pork – Talk. *'She kept rabbiting on at me.'*

Radio Ones – Runs (diarrhoea). *'I've got the Radio Ones!'*

Radio Rental – Mental. *'She's gone Radio Rental!'*

Rag and Bone – Throne (toilet). *'He's on the rag and bone.'*

Rank and Riches – Breeches. *'Are these rank and riches too tight?'*

Raspberry Ripple – Nipple. *'Look at that; you can see her raspberries!'*

Raspberry Tart – Heart. *'My raspberry belongs to you, darlin'.'*

Rr

Rat and Mouse – House. *'Went round his rat and mouse for a Ruby Murray.'*

Razor – Blazer. *'Where did you get that posh razor?'*

Read and Write – Fight. *'You been in a read and write?'*

Rhubarb Pill – Hill. *'There's a crackin' view from the rhubarb pill!'*

Rhythm and Blues – Shoes. *'I prefer Roman candles to rhythm and blues.'*

Richard Burtons – Curtains. *'Close the Richard Burtons; I'm trying to get some kip!'*

Richard the Third – Bird. *'The lad loves chatting up the Richard the Thirds.'*

River Ouse – Booze. *'You've had enough River Ouse for one night!'*

Roast Pork (shortened to Roce) – Fork. *'Don't use your fingers; use a roce!'*

Rob Roy – Boy. *'She's proud of her Rob Roy; he's in the soup and gravy.'*

Robin Hood – Good. *'That sounds Robin Hood!'*

Robinson and Cleaver – Fever. *'I'm comin' down with a Robinson.'*

Robinson Crusoe – Do So. *'He threatened to punch me so I told him to Robinson Crusoe.'*

Rock and Roll – Dole. *'He ain't worked for years – he's on the rock and roll.'*

Rock of Ages – Wages. *'I've blown my rock of ages down the rub-a-dub!'*

Rocking Horse – Sauce. *'This Ruby Murray needs more rocking horse!'*

Rolling Billows – Pillows. *'Let me plump up those rolling billows for you.'*

Rolls Royce – Voice. *'I'm losin' my Rolls Royce!'*

Rr

Roman Candles – Sandals. *'It's really hot; I'll wear my Roman candles.'*

Ronnie Barker – Marker (pen). *'Have you been drawin' on the walls with a Ronnie Barker again?'*

Rory O'Moore – Door. *'Who's that at the Rory O'Moore?'*

Rosie Lee – Tea. *'I'm gasping for a cup of Rosie!'*

Round the Houses – Trousers. *'My Scotches are too long for these round the houses!'*

Rub-a-Dub – Sub (pay advance). *'Give us a rub-a-dub till payday, guv.'*

Ruby Murray – Curry. *'This Ruby Murray'll blow your socks off!'*

Russell Harty – Party. *'It's time to Russell Harty!'*

Ss

Salmon and Trout – Gout. *'He's suffering with his salmon and trout.'*

San Toy – Boy. *'What do you want; a girl or a San Toy?'*

Santa's Grotto – Blotto. *'She's completely Santa's grotto!'*

Saucepan Handle – Candle. *'We lit some saucepan handles; it was very romantic.'*

Saucepan Lid – Kid (child). *'Shh, keep that saucepan lid quiet, will you?'*

Sausage and Mash – Cash. *'I knew his Ant 'n' Decs were dodgy, so I got him to pay me in sausage.'*

Scapa Flow – Go. *'You'd better scarper.'*

Ss

Scooby Doo – Clue. *'I don't have a Scooby.'*

Scotch Pegs – Legs. *'Slow down, my scotches are knackered!'*

Selina Scott – Spot. *'I've got a great big Selina Scott on my Harry Lin!'*

Septic Tank – Yank. *'He sounds like a septic tank.'*

Sexton Blake – Cake. *'It's your birthday, of course you'll get a Sexton Blake.'*

Shake and Shiver – River. *'She's gone and jumped in the shake and shiver!'*

Shepherd's Plaid – Bad. *'This apple's gone shepherd's plaid!'*

Sherbet Dab – Cab (taxi). *'Mind if I share your sherbet dab?'*

Sherman Tank – Yank. *'Oi, what you doin' with that Sherman tank?'*

Ship in Full Sail – Pint of Ale. *'Get that ship in full sail down you!'*

Shovel and Pick – Nick (prison). *'My skin and blister's in the shovel and nick.'*

Sieg Heils – Piles (haemorrhoids). *'I've tried every cream goin' for my Sieg Heils!'*

Sighs and Tears – Ears. *'African elephants have the biggest sighs and tears on earth.'*

Sinbad the Sailor – Tailor. *'I'm taking my suit to the Sinbad the sailor.'*

Skein of Thread – Bed. *'I'm off to skein of thread.'*

Skin and Blister – Sister. *'She may be his skin and blister but she looks nothin' like him!'*

Sky Rocket – Pocket. *'I'll put it for safekeeping in my sky rocket.'*

Ss

Small Geezers – Malteasers. *'Pop down the Cheggers and get me a bag of small geezers, would you?'*

Sorry and Sad – Bad. *'The milk's gone sorry.'*

Soup and Gravy – Navy. *'He spent twenty years in the soup and gravy.'*

St Martin's Le Grand – Hand. *'I had it in my St Martins a few minutes ago!'*

Stammer and Stutter – Butter. *'Loads of stammer and stutter for me, please.'*

Stand at Ease – Cheese. *'Wouldn't mind a stand at ease sandwich.'*

Star's Nap – Tap (ask for a loan). *'I'm going down the cab rank to ask for a star's nap.'*

Steam Tug – Mug (fool). *'I'm tired of people takin' me for a steam tug.'*

Steve Claridge – Garage. *'The car's in the Steve Claridge.'*

Stewed Prune – Tune. *'He may be a Sherman tank, but he can carry a stewed prune!'*

Sticky Toffee – Coffee. *'Is it time for a sticky toffee?'*

Stoke-on-Trent – Bent (criminal). *'I'm certain he's Stoke-on-Trent.'*

Stop Thief – Beef. *'Yorkshire pudding with your stop thief?'*

Strange and Weird – Beard. *'I'm growin' a strange and weird.'*

Strawberry Roan – Telephone. *'She's always on the strawberry.'*

Sugar and Honey – Money. *'That sweaty sock's rolling in sugar and honey!'*

Sugar Candy – Handy. *'This'll come in sugar candy.'*

Ss

Sunny South – Mouth. *'Tell him to shut his sunny south!'*

Surrey Docks – Pox. *'His daughter's got the Surrey Docks.'*

Sweaty Sock – Jock (Scotsman). *'There was an Englishman, an Irishman and a sweaty sock...'*

Sweeny Todd – Flying Squad (police). *'Here comes the Sweeny.'*

Syrup of Figs – Wig. *'I'm sure that bloke's wearin' a syrup.'*

Tt

Tartan Banner – Tanner (sixpence). *'I'm down to my last tartan.'*

Tea Leaf – Thief. *'She's always been a bit of a tea leaf.'*

Tea, Two and a Bloater – Motor. *'I've gone and locked my keys in the tea, two and a bloater!'*

Teapot Lid – Quid. *'Lend us a teapot lid, will you?'*

These and Those – Toes. *'Ouch, I've got chilblains on my these and those!'*

This and That – Cat. *'The this and that's lost his collar again!'*

Thomas Tilling – Shilling. *'I remember when it used to cost a Thomas.'*

Tt

Tick-Tock – Clock. *'What's the time on the tick-tock?'*

Tiddlywink – Drink. *'Would you like to come in for a tiddly?'*

Tin Bath – Laugh. *'You're havin' a tin bath, aren't you?'*

Tin of Fruit – Suit. *'I need a new tin of fruit for the interview.'*

Tin Tack – Sack. *'I've just got the tin tack!'*

Tin Tank – Bank. *'Won't be long, just goin' to the tin tank.'*

Tina Turner – Earner. *'It's a nice little Tina Turner.'*

Tit for Tat – Hat. *'It's too Mork and Mindy to wear a tit for tat.'*

Tit Willow – Pillow. *'Lay your head on this tit willow.'*

Todd Sloane – Alone. *'On your Todd?'*

Tom and Dick – Sick. *'I'm feelin' a bit dicky today.'*

Tom Mix – Six. *'Dinner'll be ready at Tom Mix.'*

Tom Thumb – Rum. *'A drop of Tom Thumb will make it better.'*

Tomfoolery – Jewellery. *'She's not on the floor; look at all her tomfoolery!'*

Tommy Tucker – Supper. *'Let's have a top hat over Tommy Tucker.'*

Tony Slattery – Battery. *'This Tony Slattery's gone flat!'*

Top Hat – Chat. *'Let's get together for a top hat.'*

Touch Me on the Knob – Bob (shilling). *'It'll cost you a touch me.'*

Trick Cyclist – Psychiatrist. *'I've got an appointment with my trick cyclist.'*

Tt

Trouble and Strife – Wife. *'Gotta get back to the trouble and strife.'*

Tumble Down the Sink – Drink. *'Goin' out for a tumble.'*

Turkish Bath – Laugh. *'You're havin' a Turkish.'*

Turtle Doves – Gloves. *'It's going to get two-thirty so I'd wear your turtle doves.'*

Twist and Twirl – Girl. *'As usual, the steam tug has gone to chat up a twist and twirl.'*

Two and Eight – State (anguish). *'In a bit of a two and eight.'*

Two-Thirty – Dirty. *'If it gets two-thirty I've got some band of hope in my bag.'*

Typewriter – Fighter. *'He always turns into a typewriter after too much pimple and splotch.'*

Uu

Uncle Bert – Shirt. *'Can you iron my Uncle Bert?'*

Uncle Fred – Bread. *'We're outta Uncle Fred.'*

Uncle Ned – Head. *'Use your uncle!'*

Uncle Ted – Bed. *'Have you looked under the Uncle Ted?'*

Uncle Wilf – Filth (police). *'I'm in trouble with the Uncle Wilf.'*

Uncle Willy – Silly. *'Don't be uncle.'*

Vv

Vanilla Fudge – Judge. *'If he keeps acting this way he'll end up in front of a vanilla.'*

Vera Lynns – Skins (cigarette papers). *'You got any Vera Lynns?'*

Veronica Lake – Steak. *'Do you fancy Veronica Lake and chips for tea?'*

Victoria Cross – Toss (care). *'I don't give a Victoria Cross!'*

Ww

Wallace and Gromit – Vomit. *'I think I'm gonna Wallace.'*

Weasel and Stoat – Coat. *'You'll need a weasel; it's nippy out there.'*

Weaver's Chair – Prayer. *'Say a weaver's for me.'*

Weeping Willow – Pillow. *'You need a weeping willow?'*

West Ham Reserves – Nerves. *'You're gettin' on my West Hams.'*

Westminster Abbey – Shabby. *'It's a bit Westminster if you ask me.'*

Whale and Gale – Jail. *'He's just got out of whale.'*

Ww

Whistle and Flute – Suit. *'You look sharp in that whistle and flute, mate.'*

White Mice – Ice. *'Would you like white mice with that?'*

Widow Twankey – Hanky. *'I need a Widow Twankey.'*

Wind and Kite – Website. *'I've got my own wind and kite.'*

Winona Ryder – Cider. *'I'll have a Winona.'*

Wobbly Jelly – Telly. *'Anything on the wobbly?'*

Wooden Plank – Yank. *'You're talkin' like a wooden plank.'*

Xx

There's Brussels sprout here, mate!

Yy

You and Me – Tea. *'I'll 'ave a cuppa you an' me.'*

You Must – Crust. *'Can you cut the you musts off, please?'*

Zz

Zachary Scots – Trots (diarrhoea). *'That gives me the Zacharys!'*

Zig and Zag – Shag. *'Fancy a zig and zag?'*

Zippy and Bungle – Jungle. *'He's out in the zippy at the mo.'*

If you're interested in finding out more about our books, find us on Facebook at **Summersdale Publishers** and follow us on Twitter at **@Summersdale**.

www.summersdale.com